CW00394543

Easy Fajita Cookbook

50 Delicious & Authentic Latin and Mexican Fajita Recipes

By
BookSumo Press
All rights reserved

Published by
http://www.booksumo.com

ENJOY THE RECIPES?

KEEP ON COOKING
WITH 6 MORE FREE COOKBOOKS!

Visit our website and simply enter your email address to join the club and receive your 6 cookbooks.

http://booksumo.com/magnet

https://www.instagram.com/booksumopress/

https://www.facebook.com/booksumo/

LEGAL NOTES

All Rights Reserved. No Part Of This Book May Be Reproduced Or Transmitted In Any Form Or By Any Means. Photocopying, Posting Online, And / Or Digital Copying Is Strictly Prohibited Unless Written Permission Is Granted By The Book's Publishing Company. Limited Use Of The Book's Text Is Permitted For Use In Reviews Written For The Public.

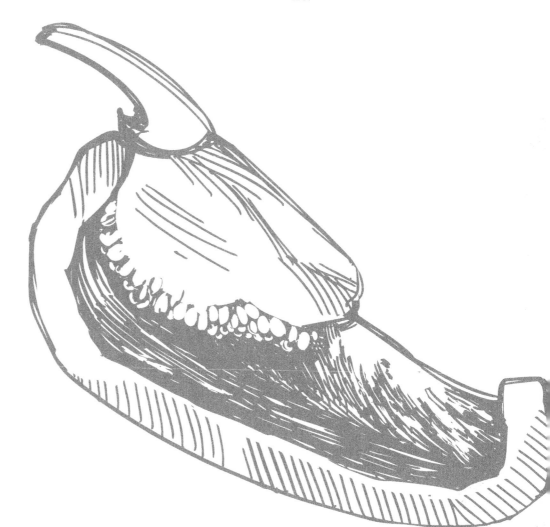

Table of Contents

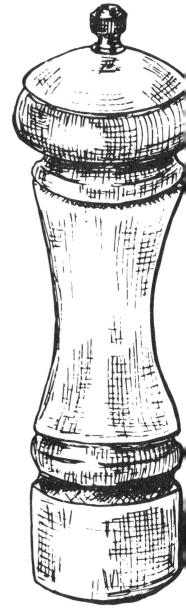

Homemade
Fajita Spice Mix

Prep Time: 5 mins
Total Time: 5 mins

Servings per Recipe: 4

Calories	21 kcal
Fat	0.4 g
Carbohydrates	4.6g
Protein	0.4 g
Cholesterol	0 mg
Sodium	596 mg

Ingredients

1 tbsp cornstarch
2 tsp chili powder
1 tsp salt
1 tsp paprika
1 tsp white sugar
1/2 tsp onion powder
1/2 tsp garlic powder

1/4 tsp cayenne pepper
1/2 tsp ground cumin

Directions

1. In a small bowl, add all the ingredients and mix well.

SNOW BELT
Fajitas

🥣 Prep Time: 30 mins
🕐 Total Time: 45 mins

Servings per Recipe: 6
Calories	688 kcal
Fat	23.2 g
Carbohydrates	78.8g
Protein	38.7 g
Cholesterol	96 mg
Sodium	1357 mg

Ingredients

Fajita Seasoning:
2 tsp seasoned salt
1/4 tsp garlic salt
1/2 tsp black pepper
1/2 tsp cayenne pepper
1 tsp dried oregano
1 1/2 lb. venison, cut into 2 inch strips

4 tbsp vegetable oil
1 medium red bell pepper, cut into 2 inch strips
1 medium yellow bell pepper, cut into 2 inch strips
1 medium onion, cut into 1/2-inch wedges
12 fajita size flour tortillas, warmed

Directions

1. For the fajita seasoning in a bowl, mix together the seasoned salt, garlic salt, black pepper, cayenne pepper and oregano.
2. Sprinkle 2 tsp of the seasoning over the sliced venison and mix well.
3. Refrigerate, covered for about 30 minutes.
4. In a heavy frying pan, heat 2 tbsp of the oil and sauté the bell pepper and onion till tender.
5. Transfer the bell pepper mixture into a bowl.
6. In the same skillet, heat the remaining oil and cook the venison till browned.
7. Add the bell pepper mixture and remaining fajita seasoning and cook till heated through.
8. Served with the warmed tortillas.

Zucchini Black Bean Veggie Fajitas

Prep Time: 20 mins
Total Time: 1 hr 10 mins

Servings per Recipe: 6
Calories	198 kcal
Fat	14.4 g
Carbohydrates	17.9 g
Protein	3 g
Cholesterol	0 mg
Sodium	130 mg

Ingredients

1/4 C. olive oil
1/4 C. red wine vinegar
1 tsp dried oregano
1 tsp chili powder
garlic salt to taste
salt and pepper to taste
1 tsp white sugar
2 small zucchini, julienned

2 medium small yellow squash, julienned
1 large onion, sliced
1 green bell pepper, cut into thin strips
1 red bell pepper, cut into thin strips
2 tbsp olive oil
1 (8.75 oz.) can whole kernel corn, drained
1 (15 oz.) can black beans, drained

Directions

1. In a large bowl mix together the olive oil, vinegar, oregano, chili powder, garlic salt, salt, pepper and sugar.
2. Add the zucchini, yellow squash, onion, green pepper and red pepper and coat with the oil mixture.
3. Refrigerate to marinate for at least 30 minutes.
4. Remove the vegetables from the refrigerator and drain well.
5. In a large skillet, heat the oil on medium-high heat and sauté the vegetables for about 10-15 minutes.
6. Stir in the corn and beans and increase the heat to high.
7. Cook for about 5 minutes.

NEW YORK
Fajitas

Prep Time: 15 mins
Total Time: 4 hr 30 mins

Servings per Recipe: 4
Calories	699 kcal
Fat	42.3 g
Carbohydrates	31.3g
Protein	49.8 g
Cholesterol	121 mg
Sodium	1451 mg

Ingredients

1/4 C. olive oil
1 lime, juiced
3 tbsp chopped fresh cilantro
2 tbsp finely chopped onion
3 cloves garlic, finely chopped
1 1/2 tsp ground cumin
1 tsp salt

1 tsp ground black pepper
2 (8 oz.) boneless New York strip steaks, cut into thin strips
8 (6 inch) white corn tortillas
1 (8 oz.) jar salsa
1 (8 oz.) package shredded Mexican cheese blend

Directions

1. In a bowl, add the olive oil, lime juice, cilantro, onion, garlic, cumin, salt and black pepper and beat till well combined.
2. Transfer the mixture into a resealable plastic bag.
3. Add the steak strips and coat with the marinade generously.
4. Squeeze out the excess air and seal the bag.
5. Refrigerate to marinate for about 4 hours to overnight.
6. Heat a large skillet over medium heat and cook the beef for 15-20 minutes.
7. Serve the cooked beef with the tortillas, salsa and Mexican cheese blend.

Mexican
Beef Marinade

Prep Time: 10 mins
Total Time: 10 mins

Servings per Recipe: 4
Calories	132 kcal
Fat	13.7 g
Carbohydrates	3g
Protein	0.4 g
Cholesterol	0 mg
Sodium	182 mg

Ingredients

1/4 C. lime juice
1/4 C. olive oil
1/3 C. water
1 tbsp vinegar
2 tsp soy sauce
2 tsp Worcestershire sauce
1 clove garlic, minced
1/2 tsp chili powder

1/2 tsp beef bouillon paste
1/2 tsp ground cumin
1/2 tsp dried oregano
1/4 tsp ground black pepper
1 pinch onion powder

Directions

1. In a bowl, add all the ingredients and beat till well combined.

MEXICAN
Quesadillas x Fajitas

🥄 Prep Time: 10 mins

🕐 Total Time: 25 mins

Servings per Recipe: 4
Calories	552 kcal
Fat	31.1 g
Carbohydrates	40g
Protein	28 g
Cholesterol	79 mg
Sodium	859 mg

Ingredients

2 tbsp vegetable oil, divided
1/2 onion, sliced
1/2 green bell pepper, sliced
salt to taste
4 flour tortillas
1/2 lb. cooked steak, cut into 1/4-inch thick pieces
1 C. shredded Mexican cheese blend

Directions

1. In a 10-inch skillet, heat 2 tsp of the oil on medium heat and sauté the onion and green bell pepper for about 5-10 minutes.
2. Stir in the salt and transfer the mixture into a bowl.
3. Brush 1 side of each tortilla with the remaining oil.
4. In the same skillet, place 1 tortilla, oil-side down on medium heat.
5. Sprinkle with 1/2 of the steak, 1/2 of the onion mixture and 1/2 of the Mexican cheese mixture.
6. Place a second tortilla, oil-side up onto the cheese layer, pressing down with a spatula to seal.
7. Cook the quesadilla for about 3-4 minutes per side.
8. Remove the quesadilla from skillet and cut into wedges.
9. Repeat with the remaining ingredients for second quesadilla.

Cinco De Mayo
Fajitas

Prep Time: 30 mins
Total Time: 50 mins

Servings per Recipe: 5
Calories	51 kcal
Fat	2.2 g
Carbohydrates	7.8g
Protein	1.7 g
Cholesterol	0 mg
Sodium	5 mg

Ingredients

2 tsp olive oil
2 cloves garlic, minced
2 green bell peppers, sliced
2 yellow bell peppers, sliced
1/2 onion, sliced
1 C. mushrooms, sliced
3 green onions, chopped
lemon pepper to taste

Directions

1. In a large frying pan over a medium heat and sauté the garlic for about 2 minutes.
2. Stir in the green and yellow bell peppers and sauté for about 2 minutes.
3. Stir in the onions and sauté for about 2 minutes.
4. Stir in the mushrooms and green onions and lemon pepper and cook, covered till the vegetables become tender.

EAST LA
Fajitas

🍳 Prep Time: 15 mins

🕐 Total Time: 2 hr 40 mins

Servings per Recipe: 4
Calories	453 kcal
Fat	21.8 g
Carbohydrates	48.1g
Protein	27.4 g
Cholesterol	38 mg
Sodium	1974 mg

Ingredients

Marinade:
4 cloves garlic
1 tbsp kosher salt
3 tbsp lime juice
3 tbsp olive oil
3 tbsp minced fresh cilantro
1 tsp chili powder
1/2 tsp white sugar
1/2 tsp paprika

1/4 tsp cayenne pepper
1 1/2 lb. beef skirt steak, cut across the grain into 1/4-inch strips
6 whole wheat tortillas
1 tbsp canola oil, divided
1 large onion, cut into slices
1 red bell pepper, cut into strips
1 clove garlic, minced
1/4 tsp salt

Directions

1. With a mortar and pestle, grind the garlic with the salt till a paste forms.
2. In a bowl, add the garlic paste, lime juice, olive oil, cilantro, chili powder, sugar, paprika and cayenne pepper and beat well.
3. Transfer the marinade into a resealable plastic bag.
4. Add the skirt steak strips and coat with the marinade.
5. Squeeze out the excess air and seal the bag.
6. Refrigerate to marinate for about 2 hours to overnight.
7. Remove the steak from marinade and shake off the excess.
8. Set your oven to 300 degrees F.
9. Wrap the tortillas tightly in aluminum foil to form a packet and arrange the packet on a baking sheet.
10. Cook in the oven for about 10 minutes.

11. Remove from the oven and keep warm.
12. In a large skillet, heat 1 tsp of the canola oil on high heat and sauté the onion and bell pepper for about 4-5 minutes.
13. Transfer the onion mixture into a plate.
14. In the same skillet, heat 1 tsp of the canola oil on high heat and cook 1/2 of the steak for about 4-6 minutes.
15. Transfer the steak into the plate with the onion mixture.
16. In the same skillet, heat the remaining canola oil and cook the remaining steak for about 4-6 minutes.
17. Stir in the minced garlic, salt, cooked steak, onion mixture and any accumulated juices and cook till fragrant and heated completely.
18. Remove from the heat and divide the steak mixture between the warm tortillas.

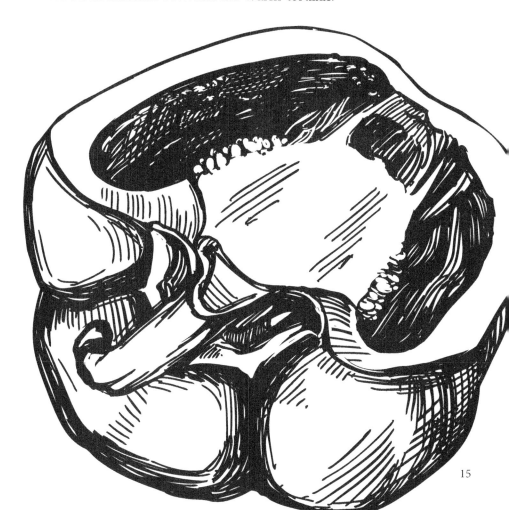

AMERICAN
Fajitas

🥣 Prep Time: 20 mins

🕐 Total Time: 2 hr 40 mins

Servings per Recipe: 4

Calories	896 kcal
Fat	37.8 g
Carbohydrates	103.9 g
Protein	37.8 g
Cholesterol	76 mg
Sodium	1182 mg

Ingredients

1 lb. lean steak, cut into strips
1/2 C. fresh lime juice
1/2 tbsp ground black pepper
1 tbsp chopped fresh cilantro
2 tbsp vegetable oil
1 large onion, cut into thin strips
1 julienned green bell pepper

2 lemons, quartered
salt and pepper to taste
6 (12 inch) flour tortillas

Directions

1. In a shallow dish, mix together the lime juice, ground pepper and cilantro.
2. Add the steak strips and coat with marinade generously.
3. Refrigerate to marinate for about 2-4 hours.
4. In a large skillet, heat 1 tbsp of the vegetable oil on medium-high heat and stir fry the steak strips till desired doneness.
5. Transfer the steak into a plate and keep aside.
6. In the same skillet, heat the remaining oil on medium-low heat and sauté the onions till tender.
7. Stir in the green peppers and steak and the juice of 1 lemon over the top and cook till the green bell peppers are just tender.
8. Remove the pan from the heat and stir in the salt and pepper.
9. Serve the steak fajitas with the tortillas and lemon wedges on the side.

Vegetarian
Fajitas

Prep Time: 15 mins
Total Time: 25 mins

Servings per Recipe: 5

Calories	424 kcal
Fat	11.3 g
Carbohydrates	67.4g
Protein	29.7 g
Cholesterol	0 mg
Sodium	924 mg

Ingredients

3 tbsp olive oil
1 red bell pepper, cut into strips
1 green bell pepper, cut into strips
1 yellow bell pepper, cut into strips
1/2 red onion, chopped
1 lb. seitan, cut into strips
2 tbsp reduced-soy sauce

3 cloves garlic, minced
1 tsp chili powder
1 tsp paprika
1 tsp ground cumin
10 whole grain tortillas

Directions

1. In a large skillet, heat the oil on medium heat and sauté the red bell pepper, green bell pepper, yellow bell pepper and onion for about 3-5 minutes.
2. Add the seitan, soy sauce, garlic, chili powder, paprika and cumin and cook for about 7-10 minutes.
3. Place the seitan filling onto each tortilla and fold the tortilla around filling.

BARBECUE PARTY
Fajitas

Prep Time: 20 mins

Total Time: 1 hr

Servings per Recipe: 6

Calories	248 kcal
Fat	16 g
Carbohydrates	5g
Protein	20.4 g
Cholesterol	49 mg
Sodium	44 mg

Ingredients

Marinade:
1/4 C. extra-virgin olive oil
1/2 lime, zested and juiced
2 cloves garlic, minced
1/2 tsp ground cumin
1/4 tsp red pepper flakes
1/4 tsp ground chipotle pepper

1 1/2 lb. beef sirloin, cut into 1-inch cubes
1 red bell pepper, cut into 1-inch cubes
1 green bell pepper, cut into 1-inch cubes
1/2 onion, cut into 1-inch cubes
skewers

Directions

1. In a large glass bowl, add the olive oil, lime juice, lime zest, garlic, cumin, red pepper flakes and chipotle pepper and beat till well combined.
2. Add the sirloin and toss to coat evenly.
3. With a plastic wrap, cover the bowl and refrigerate to marinate for about 30 minutes to 2 hours.
4. Set your outdoor grill for medium-high heat and lightly grease the grill grate.
5. Remove sirloin from the marinade and discard the excess marinade.
6. Thread the sirloin, red bell pepper, green bell pepper and onion onto skewers.
7. Cook on the grill until sirloin for about 4 minutes per side.

Cancun Cabin
Fajitas

🥣 Prep Time: 20 mins
🕐 Total Time: 45 mins

Servings per Recipe: 8
Calories	475 kcal
Fat	35.7 g
Carbohydrates	4.6g
Protein	32.8 g
Cholesterol	104 mg
Sodium	532 mg

Ingredients

3 lb. beef skirt steak
3 tsp garlic powder
3 tsp fajita seasoning
8 slices turkey bacon
1 onion, chopped
1 bell pepper, chopped
1/2 bunch cilantro, chopped

1 large tomato, chopped
10 oz. shredded Monterey Jack cheese

Directions

1. Rub the steaks with the garlic powder and fajita seasoning evenly.
2. Cut the steaks into 1 1/2-inch strips and keep aside.
3. Heat a large skillet on medium heat and cook the bacon till just crisp and brown.
4. Stir in the chopped onion, bell pepper, cilantro and steak strips and cook, stirring occasionally for about 7 minutes.
5. Stir in the tomatoes and cook till heated through.
6. Remove from the heat and serve with a topping of the Monterey Jack cheese.

ETHAN'S FAVORITE
Fajitas

🥄 Prep Time: 15 mins
🕐 Total Time: 30 mins

Servings per Recipe: 10
Calories   427 kcal
Fat   10.3 g
Carbohydrates   64.2g
Protein   18 g
Cholesterol   21 mg
Sodium   1078 mg

Ingredients

2 green bell peppers, sliced
1 red bell pepper, sliced
1 onion, thinly sliced
1 C. fresh sliced mushrooms
2 C. diced, cooked chicken meat
1 (.7 oz.) package dry Italian-style salad dressing mix
10 (12 inch) flour tortillas

Directions

1. Cut the peppers and onion into thin slices lengthwise.
2. Heat a greased skillet on low heat and sauté the peppers and onion till tender.
3. Add mushrooms and chicken and cook till heated completely.
4. Stir in the dry salad dressing mix and mix completely.
5. Warm the tortillas and roll the mixture inside.
6. If desired top with the shredded cheddar cheese, diced tomato and shredded lettuce.

Vegan
Fajitas

 Prep Time: 10 mins

Total Time: 25 mins

Servings per Recipe: 4

Calories	207 kcal
Fat	13.3 g
Carbohydrates	13.2g
Protein	12.8 g
Cholesterol	0 mg
Sodium	606 mg

Ingredients

2 tbsp corn oil
1 (8 oz.) package tempeh, broken into bite-sized pieces
2 tbsp soy sauce
1 tbsp lime juice
1 1/2 C. chopped green bell pepper
1 (4.5 oz.) can sliced mushrooms, drained

1/2 C. frozen chopped spinach, thawed and drained
1 tbsp chopped green chili peppers
1 tbsp chopped fresh cilantro
1 tbsp dried minced onion

Directions

1. In a large skillet, heat the oil on medium heat and sauté the tempeh with the soy sauce and lime juice till the tempeh browns.
2. Stir in the bell peppers, mushrooms, spinach, chili peppers, cilantro and dried onion and increase the heat to medium-high.
3. Cook, stirring occasionally till the liquid has reduced.

SIMPLY
Chicken Fajitas

Prep Time: 15 mins
Total Time: 55 mins

Servings per Recipe: 5
Calories	210 kcal
Fat	8.3 g
Carbohydrates	5.7g
Protein	27.6 g
Cholesterol	113 mg
Sodium	344 mg

Ingredients

1 tbsp Worcestershire sauce
1 tbsp cider vinegar
1 tbsp soy sauce
1 tsp chili powder
1 clove garlic, minced
1 dash hot pepper sauce
1 1/2 lb. boneless, skinless chicken thighs, cut into

strips
1 tbsp vegetable oil
1 onion, thinly sliced
1 green bell pepper, sliced
1/2 lemon, juiced

Directions

1. In a medium bowl, mix together the Worcestershire sauce, vinegar, soy sauce, chili powder, garlic and hot pepper sauce.
2. Add the chicken and coat with marinade generously.
3. Marinate for about 30 minutes at room temperature.
4. In a large skillet, heat the oil on high heat and sauté the chicken strips for about 5 minutes.
5. Add the onion and green pepper and sauté for about 3 minutes.
6. Remove from the heat and serve with the drizzling of the lemon juice.

Fajita Salad

Prep Time: 35 mins
Total Time: 35 mins

Servings per Recipe: 4

Calories	207 kcal
Fat	13.3 g
Carbohydrates	13.2g
Protein	12.8 g
Cholesterol	0 mg
Sodium	606 mg

Ingredients

8 oz. beef steak, cut into thin strips
2 tsp dry fajita seasoning
1 tbsp vegetable oil
1/2 C. sliced red or green bell peppers
1/3 C. sliced onion
1 (11 oz.) package Lettuce
1 medium tomato, diced

1/4 C. drained canned black beans
1/4 C. sliced black olives
1/4 C. shredded Cheddar cheese
Southwest Fiesta Dressing, or a chipotle dressing

Directions

1. Sprinkle the fajita seasoning over the beef strips evenly.
2. In large nonstick skillet, heat the oil on medium-high heat and stir fry the beef strips for about 3-4 minutes.
3. Add peppers and onion and sauté for about 2-3 minutes.
4. Divide the lettuce onto 2 large plates.
5. Top with the beef mixture, followed by the tomatoes, beans, olives and cheese evenly.
6. Serve with the Southwest Fiesta Dressing.

FAJITA
Soup

Prep Time: 20 mins
Total Time: 1 hr 15 mins

Servings per Recipe: 10
Calories	143 kcal
Fat	5.5 g
Carbohydrates	15.6g
Protein	12.4 g
Cholesterol	24 mg
Sodium	714 mg

Ingredients

2 tbsp vegetable oil
1 lb. skinless, boneless chicken breasts, cut into strips
1 (1.27 oz.) packet fajita seasoning
1 red bell pepper, cut into thin strips
1 green bell pepper, cut into thin strips
1 Poblano pepper, cut into thin strips
1 large onion, cut into thin strips

1 (14.5 oz.) can fire roasted diced tomatoes
1 (15 oz.) can seasoned black beans
1 (14 oz.) can chicken broth
1 dash hot sauce
salt and pepper to taste

Directions

1. In a large soup pan, heat the oil on medium heat and cook the chicken for about 10 minutes, stirring occasionally.
2. Stir in the fajita seasoning.
3. Stir in the bell peppers, Poblano pepper and onion and cook for about 10 minutes.
4. Add the fire roasted tomatoes, black beans and chicken broth and bring to a boil over high heat.
5. Reduce the heat to medium-low and simmer, uncovered for about 30 minutes, stirring occasionally.
6. Season the soup with the hot sauce, salt and pepper before serving.

Fajitas
101

Prep Time: 15 mins
Total Time: 30 mins

Servings per Recipe: 4
Calories	391 kcal
Fat	13.9 g
Carbohydrates	46.5g
Protein	21.6 g
Cholesterol	31 mg
Sodium	1068 mg

Ingredients

Tacos:
1 tbsp vegetable oil
1 (1 oz.) package Old El Paso(R) taco seasoning mix
1 (1 1/4 lb.) flank steak, trimmed of excess fat
8 (6 inch) Old El Paso(R) flour tortillas for soft tacos
& fajitas
Mango Salsa:

2 ripe medium mangoes, seed removed, peeled
and diced
Juice of 1 medium lime
1 jalapeno chili, seeded, chopped
1/4 C. chopped red onion
1/4 C. chopped fresh cilantro leaves

Directions

1. Set your oven to 400 degrees F before doing anything else and line a baking sheet with the foil paper.
2. Sprinkle taco seasoning mix over flank steak, pressing to coat.
3. In a 10-inch skillet, heat the oil on high heat and sear the steak till browned from both sides.
4. Place the steak onto the prepared baking sheet.
5. Cook in the oven till the meat thermometer inserted in center of steak reads 135 degrees F.
6. Remove from the oven and keep aside for about 10 minutes.
7. Meanwhile in large bowl, mix together the salsa ingredients and refrigerate before serving.
8. Cut the steak into thin slices.
9. Place 2-3 slices of the steak on each tortilla and top with the salsa.
10. Roll up the tortillas and serve.

FAJITA
Town

Prep Time: 15 mins

Total Time: 6 hr 30 mins

Servings per Recipe: 3
Calories	501 kcal
Fat	27.9 g
Carbohydrates	38g
Protein	23.2 g
Cholesterol	34 mg
Sodium	925 mg

Ingredients

1 lb. beef flank steak
1/4 C. vegetable oil
3 tbsp lime juice
1 (1 oz.) package ranch dressing mix
1/4 tsp ground cumin
1/2 tsp ground black pepper
3 (8 inch) flour tortillas

1/2 onion, sliced
1/2 green bell pepper, sliced

Directions

1. With a fork, pierce the flank steak evenly and place into a large resealable plastic zipper bag.
2. In a bowl, mix together the vegetable oil, lime juice, ranch dressing mix, cumin and black pepper.
3. Place the mixture over the flank steak.
4. Squeeze out the excess air and seal the bag.
5. Refrigerate to marinate for at least 6 hours.
6. Set your outdoor grill for medium-high heat and lightly grease the grill grate.
7. Remove the flank steak from the marinade and shake off the excess marinade.
8. Cook the steak on grill for about 10 minutes, basting with the marinade occasionally.
9. Remove the steak from the grill and keep aside for about 10 minutes before slicing thinly on the diagonal.
10. Meanwhile cook the onion on grill the onion and green pepper slices for about 3 minutes per side.
11. Wrap the sliced steak with grilled onion and green pepper in the tortillas.

Maria's
Fajitas

🥣 Prep Time: 30 mins

🕐 Total Time: 12 hr 55 mins

Servings per Recipe: 8

Calories	506 kcal
Fat	15.4 g
Carbohydrates	68.7g
Protein	22.8 g
Cholesterol	32 mg
Sodium	1006 mg

Ingredients

1 lb. skinless, boneless chicken breast halves
Marinade:
2 tbsp soy sauce
1 tbsp lime juice
1 tbsp honey
1/2 small jalapeno pepper, seeded and minced
1 clove garlic, minced
Guacamole:
1 avocado, peeled and pitted
1 tomato, peeled and chopped

1/2 C. minced onion
1 tbsp lime juice
1 tbsp chopped fresh cilantro
1 dash hot pepper sauce
2 tsp canola oil
1 onion, thinly sliced
1/2 red bell pepper, thinly sliced
8 (12 inch) flour tortillas
1 C. shredded lettuce

Directions

1. In a large glass bowl, place the chicken.
2. In another bowl, add the soy sauce, 1 tbsp lime juice, honey, jalapeño pepper and garlic and beat till smooth.
3. Place the marinade over the chicken and toss to coat well.
4. With a plastic wrap, cover the bowl and refrigerate for about 12 hours to overnight, flipping occasionally.
5. Remove the chicken from marinade and shake off the excess.
6. Place the remaining marinade into a small pan and bring to a boil.
7. Reduce the heat to medium-low and simmer for about 5 minutes.
8. In a bowl, add the avocado and mash well.

9. Add the tomato, minced onion, 1 tbsp of lime juice, cilantro and hot pepper sauce and mix till the guacamole is well combined.
10. Set your outdoor grill for medium-high heat and lightly grease the grill grate.
11. Cook the chicken on grill for about 7-15 minutes, flipping occasionally and basting with the marinade.
12. Transfer the chicken into a plate and cover with a foil paper for about 5 minutes.
13. Slice the chicken across the grain into thin strips.
14. In a large nonstick skillet, heat the oil on medium-high heat and sauté the sliced onion and red bell pepper for about 10 minutes.
15. Wrap the tortillas in a damp paper towel and microwave on high for about 1-3 minutes.
16. Place chicken strips in the center of each tortilla and top with the shredded lettuce, sautéed onion and red bell peppers and guacamole.
17. Wrap each tortilla tightly around the filling.

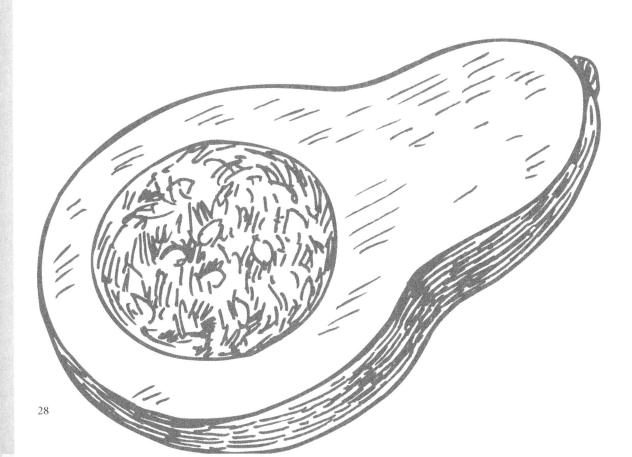

Wednesday's
Dinner Fajitas

Prep Time: 10 mins
Total Time: 25 mins

Servings per Recipe: 6

Calories	547 kcal
Fat	25.5 g
Carbohydrates	62.1g
Protein	25.5 g
Cholesterol	100 mg
Sodium	2638 mg

Ingredients

2 tbsp vegetable oil
2 onions, sliced
2 sweet peppers, sliced
1/2 tsp salt
1/2 tsp pepper
1 lb. ground turkey
2 cloves garlic, minced
2 tsp chili powder

1 1/2 C. Heinz(R) Chili Sauce, Chunky with Sweet Peppers
2 tbsp Heinz Tomato Ketchup
2 (10 inch) flour tortillas
1 1/2 C. shredded old Cheddar cheese
2 C. shredded lettuce
2/3 C. low-fat sour cream

Directions

1. In a skillet, heat half of the oil on medium-high heat and sauté the onions, peppers and half of the salt and pepper for about 5 minutes.
2. Transfer the onion mixture in a bowl and keep aside.
3. In the same skillet, heat the remaining oil and stir fry the turkey, garlic, chili powder and remaining salt and pepper for about 5 minutes.
4. Stir in half of the chili sauce and all of the ketchup and bring to a simmer.
5. Serve the turkey and vegetable mixtures with the tortillas and bowls of remaining chili sauce, cheese, lettuce and sour cream.

FLORIDA ORANGE
Fajitas

Prep Time: 10 mins
Total Time: 1 d 20 mins

Servings per Recipe: 4

Calories	155 kcal
Fat	8.6 g
Carbohydrates	5.1g
Protein	13.9 g
Cholesterol	36 mg
Sodium	258 mg

Ingredients

2 oranges, juiced
1 tbsp ground cumin
1 chipotle chili pepper, minced
1/2 tsp sea salt
1 lb. skirt steak

Directions

1. In a bowl, add the orange juice, cumin, chili pepper and sea salt and beat well.
2. Transfer the mixture into a resealable plastic bag with the steak and shake to coat.
3. Squeeze out the excess air and seal the bag.
4. Refrigerate to marinate for about 24 hours.
5. Set your outdoor grill for medium-high heat and lightly grease the grill grate.
6. Remove the steak from marinade and discard the marinade.
7. Cook the steak on grill for about 3-4 minutes per side.

Classical Latin
Fajita Marinade

Prep Time: 5 mins
Total Time: 5 mins

Servings per Recipe: 6
Calories	36 kcal
Fat	0.1 g
Carbohydrates	7.6g
Protein	1.6 g
Cholesterol	0 mg
Sodium	1204 mg

Ingredients

1 C. pineapple juice
1/2 C. soy sauce
2 tbsp fresh lime juice
1 tsp ground cumin
1/2 tsp minced garlic

Directions

1. In a bowl, add all ingredients and beat well.
2. This marinade will marinate up to 2 lb. of meat for at least 4 hours before using.

SAINT ANNA'S
Fajitas

Prep Time: 10 mins
Total Time: 2 h 20 mins

Servings per Recipe: 6

Calories	547 kcal
Fat	25.5 g
Carbohydrates	62.1g
Protein	25.5 g
Cholesterol	100 mg
Sodium	2638 mg

Ingredients

3 lb. flank or skirt steak, cut against the grain into 1/2-inch thick strips
1 1/2 C. Goya Mojo Criollo
1 tsp Goya Adobo with Pepper
2 tbsp Goya Extra Virgin Olive Oil
1 large yellow onion, cut into 1/4-inch strips
2 red, green, and/or yellow bell peppers, cut into 1/4-inch thick strips

1 tsp Goya Sazonador Total
1 (18 oz.) package Goya Flour Tortillas, warmed
For the garnish:
1 (12 oz.) container Goya Guacamole, thawed
1 (17.6 oz.) jar Goya Salsa Pico de Gallo
1 C. sour cream
1 (8 oz.) jar Goya Salsita (preferred flavor)

Directions

1. In a large Ziploc bag, mix together the steak slices, Mojo and 1 tsp of the Adobo.
2. Refrigerate to marinate for at least 2 hours or up to 24 hours.
3. Discard the marinade and bring the steak to room temperature.
4. In a large skillet, heat 1 tbsp. of the oil on high heat and sauté the onions for about 3 minutes.
5. Stir in the peppers and cook, stirring occasionally for about 3 minutes.
6. Season vegetables with the sazonador total and adobo.
7. Transfer the vegetables into large serving platter and cover with a foil paper to keep warm.
8. In the same skillet, heat the remaining oil on high heat and cook the beef in batches for about 10 minutes.
9. Transfer the beef into serving platter.
10. Place the beef and vegetables into center of warm tortillas and top with the guacamole, pico de gallo, sour cream and salsita.
11. Wrap and enjoy.

Fajitas

🥣 Prep Time: 25 mins

🕐 Total Time: 10 h 25 mins

Servings per Recipe: 6
Calories	504 kcal
Fat	26.9 g
Carbohydrates	36.5g
Protein	28.3 g
Cholesterol	87 mg
Sodium	530 mg

Ingredients

1 (2 1/2 lb.) beef chuck roast, trimmed
1 large onion, chopped
1 (14.5 oz.) can Del Monte(R) Original Stewed Tomatoes (undrained), chopped
1 (4 oz.) can diced green chilis
4 cloves garlic, minced
2 tsp ground cumin
1 tsp dried oregano
1/2 tsp cayenne pepper
1 tbsp vegetable oil
2 green or yellow bell peppers, cut into bite-size strips
1 large onion, cut into thin wedges
1 (14.5 oz.) can Del Monte(R) Original Stewed Tomatoes, drained and coarsely chopped
6 (8 inch) flour tortillas, warmed*
Sour cream
Guacamole
Salsa
Lime wedges

Directions

1. Cut the beef in 2-inch pieces.
2. In a large slow cooker, place the chopped onion and top with the beef.
3. In a bowl, mix together 1 can of the undrained stewed tomatoes, green chilis, garlic, cumin, oregano and cayenne pepper.
4. Place the mixture over the beef in slow cooker.
5. Set the slow cooker on Low and cook, covered for about 10-12 hours.
6. With a slotted spoon, transfer the beef into a large bowl.
7. With two forks, shred the beef and cover to keep warm.
8. In a large skillet, heat the oil on medium-high heat and sauté the bell peppers and onion wedges for about 4-5 minutes.
9. Stir in the remaining can of the stewed tomatoes and cook till heated completely.
10. Place about 1/2 C. of the beef and 1/2 C. of the pepper mixture onto one side of each warmed tortilla.
11. Fold the tortilla in half over the filling.
12. Top with the sour cream, guacamole and salsa.
13. Serve with lime wedges.

SEPTEMBER'S
Fajitas

Prep Time: 10 mins

Total Time: 3 h 30 mins

Servings per Recipe: 6
Calories	257 kcal
Fat	18.8 g
Carbohydrates	7.7g
Protein	14.1 g
Cholesterol	34 mg
Sodium	1101 mg

Ingredients

1/2 C. olive oil
1/2 C. distilled white vinegar
1/2 C. fresh lime juice
2 (.7 oz.) packages dry Italian-style salad dressing mix
3 whole boneless, skinless chicken breast, cubed
1 onion, sliced

1 green bell pepper, sliced

Directions

1. In a large glass bowl mix together the oil, vinegar, lime juice and dry salad dressing mix.
2. Add the chicken strips, onion and bell pepper and coat with the mixture.
3. Refrigerate, covered to marinate for about 3-6 hours.
4. Remove the chicken, onion and bell pepper from the marinade.
5. In a large skillet, heat the oil and cook the chicken, onion and bell pepper till done completely.

Mas Maiz
Fajitas

🍳 Prep Time: 15 mins
🕐 Total Time: 25 mins

Servings per Recipe: 4

Calories	547 kcal
Fat	17.8 g
Carbohydrates	60.8g
Protein	34.9 g
Cholesterol	69 mg
Sodium	824 mg

Ingredients

2 tbsp Mazola(R) Corn Oil
1 lb. chicken breast tenders
1 medium onion, cut into julienne strips
2 green or red bell peppers, cut into julienne strips
1 tsp Spice Islands(R) Oregano
1 tsp Spice Islands(R) Garlic Salt
3/4 tsp Spice Islands(R) Ground Cumin

8 (6- to 8-inch) tortillas, warmed

Directions

1. In a large skillet, heat the oil on medium heat and stir fry the chicken, onion, and pepper for about 3-5 minutes.
2. Stir in the oregano, garlic salt, cumin, salt and pepper.
3. Fill the warm tortillas with the chicken mixture.
4. Serve with a garnishing of the sour cream, avocado, cilantro and lime wedges.

RED WHITE AND GREEN
Fajitas

🥘 Prep Time: 10 mins
🕐 Total Time: 45 mins

Servings per Recipe: 8
Calories   370 kcal
Fat   10.4 g
Carbohydrates   50.2g
Protein   14.8 g
Cholesterol   24 mg
Sodium   564 mg

Ingredients

2 tbsp oil, divided
1 lb. boneless beef sirloin steak, cut into thin strips
1 medium onion, thinly sliced
1 medium green bell pepper, thinly sliced
1 (6.9 oz.) package boxed Spanish Rice, or dirty rice
1 1/2 C. water
1 (14.5 oz.) can diced tomatoes, undrained
8 (8 inch) flour tortillas

Directions

1. In a large nonstick skillet, heat 1 tbsp of the oil on medium-high heat and sear the beef for about 3-5 minutes.
2. Transfer the beef into a bowl.
3. In the same skillet, heat the remaining 1 tbsp of the oil and cook the vegetables for about 2 minutes.
4. Transfer the vegetable mixture into the bowl with the beef and keep warm.
5. In the same skillet, mix together the Rice Mix, water and tomatoes and bring to a boil.
6. Reduce the heat to low and simmer, covered for about 25 minutes.
7. Stir in the beef and vegetables and cook till heated completely.
8. Serve in the warmed tortillas.

Summertime Fajitas

Prep Time: 15 mins
Total Time: 25 mins

Servings per Recipe: 4
Calories	410 kcal
Fat	10 g
Carbohydrates	46.3g
Protein	32.2 g
Cholesterol	66 mg
Sodium	709 mg

Directions

1. Set your oven to 350 degrees F before doing anything else.
2. Wrap the tortillas in aluminum foil and heat in the oven.
3. In a large bowl, mix together the chicken, bell pepper, jerk seasoning and pepper and keep aside.
4. Coat a large skillet with cooking spray and heat on medium-high heat.
5. Add the pineapple and cook for about 4-6 minutes.
6. Remove the pineapple from the pan and keep aside.
7. In the same skillet, heat the vegetable oil and cook the chicken and peppers for about 6 minutes.
8. Stir in the cooked pineapple.
9. Serve in the warmed tortillas and serve with a squeeze of the lime juice and garnishing of the cilantro.

Ingredients

8 (6 inch) flour tortillas
1 lb. skinless, boneless chicken breast halves - cut into strips
2 small red bell peppers, cut into strips
2 tsp Jamaican jerk seasoning
1/8 tsp ground black pepper
4 slices canned pineapple, chopped
1 tbsp vegetable oil
chopped fresh cilantro
lime wedges

EL AGUILA
Fajitas

🥣 Prep Time: 10 mins

🕐 Total Time: 25 mins

Servings per Recipe: 6

Calories	348 kcal
Fat	9.6 g
Carbohydrates	44.7g
Protein	18.8 g
Cholesterol	115 mg
Sodium	1012 mg

Ingredients

1 1/2 tbsp vegetable oil, divided
1 green bell pepper, sliced
1 red bell pepper, sliced
1 lb. medium shrimp - peeled and deveined
1 C. (1 small) chopped onion
1 (1.25 oz.) package taco seasoning mix
3 tbsp water, or as needed

6 (10 inch) flour tortillas, warmed

Directions

1. In a large skillet, heat 1 tbsp of the oil on medium-high heat and sauté the bell peppers and onion for about 5 minutes.
2. Transfer the bell pepper mixture into a bowl and keep aside.
3. In the same skillet, heat the remaining 1/2 tbsp of the oil and cook the shrimp. Cook the shrimp till pink and opaque, stirring occasionally.
4. Reduce the heat to low and stir in the peppers mixture, taco seasoning and water and simmer till heated completely.
5. Serve in the warm tortillas.

Tijuana
Fajitas

Prep Time: 20 mins
Total Time: 2 hr 35 mins

Servings per Recipe: 4
Calories	168 kcal
Fat	4.7 g
Carbohydrates	10.6g
Protein	15 g
Cholesterol	25 mg
Sodium	601 mg

Ingredients

1 lb. trimmed skirt steak
(12 oz.) broth
1/3 C. freshly squeezed key-lime juice
1 onion, cut into rings
1 large green bell pepper, cut into rings
1 tsp onion powder
1 tsp lemon pepper seasoning

1 tsp garlic powder
1 tsp garlic salt

Directions

1. In a glass bowl, mix together the broth, lime juice, onion and bell pepper.
2. With a meat mallet, pound the skirt steaks to 1/4-inch thickness.
3. Add the steaks into the bowl with the marinade and mix well.
4. With a plastic wrap, cover the bowl and refrigerate to marinate for about 2 hours.
5. Set your outdoor grill for medium-high heat and lightly grease the grill grate.
6. Remove the skirt steak from the marinade and discard the remaining marinade.
7. In a small bowl, mix together the onion powder, lemon pepper, garlic powder and garlic salt.
8. Season the steaks with the spice mixture evenly.
9. Cook the steaks on the grill for about 7 minutes per side.

POTLUCK
Fajitas II

Prep Time: 30 mins
Total Time: 50 mins

Servings per Recipe: 4
Calories   257 kcal
Fat   12.6 g
Carbohydrates   19.7g
Protein   17.4 g
Cholesterol   49 mg
Sodium   136 mg

Ingredients

2 skinless, boneless chicken breast halves, cut into 1/4-inch wide strips
1 lime, juiced
1/2 tsp ground cumin
1/4 tsp paprika
1/4 tsp chili powder
1/8 tsp cayenne pepper
1/8 tsp ground black pepper
1 tbsp olive oil

1 red bell pepper, cut into 1/4 inch strips
1/2 large red onion, sliced 1/4-inch thick
4 (6 inch) corn tortillas
1/4 C. sour cream, divided
1/2 C. shredded Cheddar-Monterey Jack cheese blend, divided
1 C. shredded lettuce, divided
1/2 C. diced tomato, divided

Directions

1. In a large bowl, mix together the chicken strips, lime juice, cumin, paprika, chili powder, cayenne pepper and black pepper.
2. Marinate the chicken for about 15-30 minutes.
3. In a large skillet, heat the oil on medium heat and sauté the red bell pepper and onion for about 5 minutes.
4. Move the vegetables to the sides of the skillet.
5. Place chicken strips with marinade in the center of the skillet and cook for about 3 minutes.
6. Stir the chicken with the vegetables and cook for about 2 minutes.
7. Remove from the heat and keep aside.
8. In a microwave-safe plate, place the corn tortillas with damp paper towels separating each tortilla

and microwave for about 30 seconds.

9. Arrange the corn tortillas onto 4 serving plates and spread 1 tbsp of the sour cream over each tortilla.
10. Top each tortilla with 1/4 of the chicken mixture, followed by 2 tbsp of the shredded Cheddar-Monterey Jack cheese blend, 1/4 C. of the lettuce and 2 tbsp of the diced tomato.
11. Repeat with the remaining tortillas and ingredients.
12. Top with the desired toppings and serve.

CATALINA'S
Secret Fajitas

Prep Time: 10 mins
Total Time: 1 hr

Servings per Recipe: 12
Calories	112 kcal
Fat	7.2 g
Carbohydrates	4.3g
Protein	7.3 g
Cholesterol	18 mg
Sodium	20 mg

Ingredients

1/4 C. lime juice
1/4 C. chopped fresh cilantro
1/2 jalapeno pepper, seeded and minced
2 tbsp olive oil
2 cloves garlic, minced
1 tsp ground cumin
1 1/2 lb. beef skirt steak, cut across the grain into

1/2-inch strips
1 yellow onion, cut into 1/2-inch strips
3 red bell peppers, cut into 1/2-inch strips
2 tsp vegetable oil, divided

Directions

1. In a large glass bowl, add the lime juice, cilantro, jalapeño pepper, olive oil, garlic and cumin and beat well.
2. Add the skirt steak, onion and red bell peppers and toss to coat evenly.
3. With a plastic wrap, cover the bowl and marinate to refrigerator for about 30 minutes to 2 hours.
4. Remove the steak, onion, and peppers from marinade and shake off the excess.
5. Discard remaining marinade.
6. In a large skillet, heat 1 tsp of the vegetable oil on high heat and sear the steak for about 3 minutes per side.
7. Transfer the steak into a plate and cover with a foil paper for about 5 minutes.
8. In the same skillet, heat the remaining oil on medium-high heat and sauté the onion and peppers for about 5-6 minutes.
9. Stir in the steak and cook till heated completely.

Zucchini
Fajita Bake

🥣 Prep Time: 30 mins

🕐 Total Time: 1 hr 25 mins

Servings per Recipe: 8

Calories	457 kcal
Fat	11.2 g
Carbohydrates	77.4g
Protein	20.5 g
Cholesterol	2 mg
Sodium	1678 mg

Ingredients

1/2 zucchini, cut into 1/4-inch slices
1 C. red bell pepper slices
1 onion, cut into 1/4-inch slices and separated into rings
1 C. water
1 tsp vegetable oil
1 (1.27 oz.) packet dry fajita seasoning
1/2 C. all-purpose flour
1/2 C. nutritional yeast
1 tsp salt
1 1/2 tsp garlic powder
1/2 tsp dry mustard powder
2 C. water
1/4 C. margarine

2 (10 oz.) cans red enchilada sauce
5 (9 inch) whole-wheat tortillas, torn into 1-inch pieces
1 1/2 C. cooked brown rice
3 (15 oz.) cans black beans, rinsed and drained
1 tbsp sliced black olives (optional)
1/4 avocado - peeled, pitted and diced (optional)
2 tbsp chopped tomato (optional)
1 jalapeno pepper, seeded and thinly sliced (optional)
2 tbsp chopped onion (optional)
2 tbsp prepared salsa (optional)
2 tbsp sour cream (optional)

Directions

1. Set your oven to 350 degrees F before doing anything else.
2. In a large bowl, mix together the zucchini, red bell pepper, and 1 onion, 1 C. of the water, vegetable oil and dry fajita seasoning.
3. Marinate for about 1-2 hours then drain the vegetables.
4. Heat a large skillet on medium heat and cook the vegetables for about 10 minutes.
5. Transfer the vegetables into a bowl and keep aside.

6. In a pan, place the flour, nutritional yeast, salt, garlic powder, dry mustard powder and 2 C. of the water and beat till well combined.
7. Place the pan on medium heat and bring to a boil.
8. Reduce the heat to low and simmer for about 5 minutes, beating continuously.
9. Stir in the margarine and remove from the heat.
10. Spread 1/2 can of enchilada sauce in the bottom of a 13x9-inch baking dish evenly.
11. Top with 1/4 of the tortilla pieces, followed by 1/2 C. of the brown rice.
12. Place 1/3 of the cooked vegetables over the brown rice.
13. Spread 1 can of the black beans over the vegetables and top with 1/4 of the nutritional yeast sauce evenly.
14. Repeat the layers twice.
15. Make a final layer with the remaining 1/4 of the tortilla pieces, remaining nutritional yeast sauce and remaining 1/2 can of the enchilada sauce.
16. Cook in the oven for about 30-45 minutes.
17. Remove from the oven and keep aside for about 10 minutes.
18. Top the casserole with the black olives, avocado, tomato, jalapeño pepper, 2 tbsp of chopped onion, salsa and sour cream before serving.

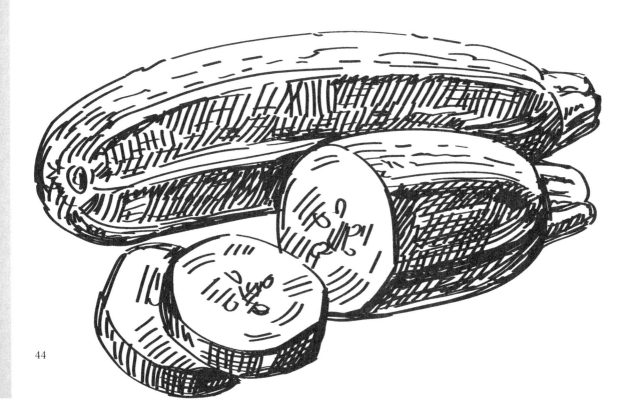

Lumberjack
Fajitas

Prep Time: 25 mins
Total Time: 2 hr 50 mins

Servings per Recipe: 6

Calories	357 kcal
Fat	29.2 g
Carbohydrates	4.6g
Protein	14.1 g
Cholesterol	39 mg
Sodium	235 mg

Ingredients

1 1/2 lb. beef round steak
1/4 C. tequila, or beef broth
1/2 C. fresh lime juice
1/2 C. cooking oil
2 tbsp liquid smoke
1 tsp Worcestershire sauce
1/4 tsp ground black pepper

1/2 tsp salt
3/4 tsp paprika
1/2 C. sliced onion
3/4 C. bell peppers, sliced into thin strips

Directions

1. In a plastic bag, mix together the steak, tequila and lime juice and refrigerate to marinate for about 2 hours.
2. Set your outdoor grill for high heat and lightly grease the grill grate.
3. Remove the steak from the bag and discard the marinade.
4. Cook the steak on grill for about 8 minutes per side.
5. Remove the steak from the grill and slice into 1/4-inch strips.
6. In a serving plate, arrange the strips.
7. In a skillet, heat the oil on medium heat.
8. Stir in the liquid smoke, Worcestershire sauce, pepper, salt and paprika to the oil and heat the mixture.
9. Add the onions and peppers and cook till the peppers become tender.
10. Place the mixture over the steak strips and serve immediately.

THURSDAY'S
Stovetop Fajitas

Prep Time: 10 mins
Total Time: 20 mins

Servings per Recipe: 4	
Calories	518 kcal
Fat	14.1 g
Carbohydrates	60.1g
Protein	34.1 g
Cholesterol	69 mg
Sodium	1117 mg

Ingredients

1 tbsp vegetable oil
1 lb. boneless, skinless chicken breasts, thinly sliced
1 (14 oz.) bag Birds Eye(R) Recipe Ready Tri-Color
Pepper & Onion Blend
1 tsp ground cumin or fajita seasoning blend
1 tsp salt
8 flour tortillas, warmed

Directions

1. In a large nonstick skillet, heat oil on medium-high heat and cook the chicken for about 5 minutes, stirring occasionally.
2. Stir in the Recipe Ready Tri-Color Peppers & Onions Blend, cumin and salt and cook for about 5 minutes, stirring occasionally.
3. Serve in the flour tortillas and serve with a garnishing of the lime wedges.

Celebration Mexican
Fajita Marinade

🍳 Prep Time: 15 mins

🕐 Total Time: 1 d 15 mins

Servings per Recipe: 8

Calories	457 kcal
Fat	11.2 g
Carbohydrates	77.4g
Protein	20.5 g
Cholesterol	2 mg
Sodium	1678 mg

Ingredients

3 limes, juiced
2 green onions, chopped
3 cloves garlic, minced
3 tbsp chopped fresh cilantro
2 tbsp vegetable oil
1/2 tsp red pepper flakes
1/4 tsp ground coriander

1/4 tsp ground anise seed (optional)

Directions

1. In a bowl, add all the ingredients and mix till well combined.
2. Pour mixture over your favorite meat.
3. Refrigerate, covered to marinate for about 12-24 hours before cooking as desired.

ARIZONA
Southwest Fajitas

Prep Time: 15 mins
Total Time: 55 mins

Servings per Recipe: 6
Calories   395 kcal
Fat   12.9 g
Carbohydrates   49.5g
Protein   22.3 g
Cholesterol   45 mg
Sodium   1234 mg

Ingredients

4 boneless, skinless chicken breast halves
1 tbsp ground cinnamon
salt and pepper to taste
2 large baking potatoes, peeled and cubed
1/4 C. canola oil
1 large yellow onion, chopped
1 large clove garlic, peeled and minced

1 tbsp chopped jalapeno peppers
1 lime, juiced
12 (6 inch) corn tortillas, warmed

Directions

1. Set your oven to 400 degrees F before doing anything else.
2. In a shallow baking dish, place the potatoes.
3. Drizzle with about 1/2 of the oil and sprinkle with the salt evenly.
4. Cook in the oven for about 30 - 40 minutes.
5. Meanwhile season the chicken with the cinnamon, salt and pepper.
6. In another baking dish, place the chicken breast halves and cook in the oven for about 30 minutes.
7. Remove from the oven and let it cool.
8. After cooling, shred the chicken breast halves.
9. In a skillet, heat the remaining oil on medium heat and sauté the onion and garlic till tender.
10. Stir in the shredded chicken, jalapeño and lime juice and cook till heated completely.
11. Serve the chicken and potatoes in warmed tortillas.

Fun
Fajitas

Prep Time: 15 mins
Total Time: 25 mins

Servings per Recipe: 4
Calories   355 kcal
Fat   18.6 g
Carbohydrates   43.4g
Protein   17.4 g
Cholesterol   30 mg
Sodium   456 mg

Directions

1. In a bowl, add the garlic, jalapeño, cumin, cilantro, lime juice, sugar and oil and beat till well combined.
2. Transfer the marinade into a plastic gallon-size zip top bag.
3. Add the flank steak and refrigerate to marinate for about 1-4 hours.
4. In a platter, assemble the tomatoes, cheese and lettuce leaves.
5. Set your grill for medium-high heat and arrange an 8-inch cast iron pan directly on the grill.
6. Remove the steak from the marinade, and pat dry with the paper towel.
7. Season with the salt and pepper.
8. Cook the steak on grill for about 6-8 minutes per side.
9. Remove from the grill and keep aside for about 5 minutes before slicing into 1/2-inch thick slices.
10. Meanwhile, grease a preheated cast iron pan with non-stick spray.
11. Add the corn, red onion and Poblano peppers and sauté for about 6-8 minutes.
12. At the same time, coat the tortillas with non-stick spray.
13. Cook the tortillas on grill for about 30 seconds from both sides.
14. Immediately place the sliced steak on top of the corn mixture in cast iron pan and serve sizzling hot.

Ingredients

4 Mission(R) Soft Taco Flour Tortillas
2 cloves garlic, minced
1/2 jalapeno pepper, minced
1/2 tsp ground cumin
1/4 C. cilantro, chopped
2 limes, juiced
1 tsp sugar
2 tbsp olive oil
1 (12 oz.) flank steak
1/2 C. tomatoes, cut into large chunks
1 tbsp crumbled cotija cheese
4 Bibb lettuce leaves
Salt and pepper as needed
1 C. frozen sweet corn kernels
1/2 C. red onion, diced
1 Poblano pepper, cut into strips

MEXICO CITY
Fajitas

Prep Time: 10 mins
Total Time: 35 mins

Servings per Recipe: 8

Calories	397 kcal
Fat	16.6 g
Carbohydrates	19.9g
Protein	40.3 g
Cholesterol	104 mg
Sodium	821 mg

Ingredients

3 tbsp vegetable oil
6 (6 oz.) skinless, boneless chicken breast halves, thinly sliced
1/2 C. sliced onions
1/2 C. sliced red bell pepper
1/2 C. tomato juice
2 tbsp taco seasoning mix

1 C. salsa
8 (1/2 inch thick) slices French bread
2 C. shredded Cheddar cheese

Directions

1. In a large skillet, heat the oil on medium-high heat and cook the chicken for about 5 minutes.
2. Stir in the sliced onions and red peppers and cook for about 5 minutes.
3. Stir in the tomato juice and taco seasoning and cook for about 7 minutes.
4. Set the broiler of your oven and arrange oven rack about 6-inches from the heating element.
5. Spread 2 tbsp of salsa over each slice of French bread and top with the chicken mixture evenly.
6. Sprinkle each sandwich with 1/4 C. of the Cheddar cheese.
7. Cook the sandwiches under the broiler for about 5 minutes.

Sun-Belt
Bison Fajitas

🥣 Prep Time: 30 mins
🕐 Total Time: 2 hr 42 mins

Servings per Recipe: 6

Calories	456 kcal
Fat	23.5 g
Carbohydrates	43.9 g
Protein	20.9 g
Cholesterol	39 mg
Sodium	518 mg

Ingredients

1 lb. bison flank steak
1 1/2 tsp fajita seasoning
2 tbsp vegetable oil
2 cloves garlic, minced
1 fresh jalapeno pepper, seeded and chopped
1 large onion, thinly sliced
1 large green bell pepper, thinly sliced
1 large red or yellow bell pepper, thinly sliced
6 (8 inch) flour tortillas, warmed
Salsa
Sour cream

Lime wedges
Guacamole Salad:
2 Roma tomatoes, seeded and chopped
3 tbsp sliced green onions
1 fresh jalapeno pepper, seeded and chopped
2 cloves garlic, minced
1/2 tsp salt
1/4 tsp black pepper
2 large ripe avocados, halved, seeded, peeled, and coarsely mashed
Shredded romaine lettuce

Directions

1. Thinly slice the bison flank steak across the grain into bite-size strips and sprinkle with 1 tsp of the fajita seasoning.
2. Cover and chill for about 30 minutes.
3. In a large skillet, heat 1 tbsp of the oil on medium-high heat and sauté the garlic and the 1 jalapeño pepper for about 2 minutes.
4. Add the onion and sauté for about 6-8 minutes.
5. Transfer the onion mixture into a medium bowl.
6. Cover and keep warm.
7. In the same skillet, add the bell peppers and remaining 1/2 tsp of the fajita seasoning and cook for

about 6 - 8 minutes.

8. Transfer the peppers into the bowl with onion mixture.
9. Cover and keep warm.
10. In the same skillet, heat the remaining 1 tbsp of the oil and cook 1/2 of the bison flank steak strips for about 1 - 2 minutes.
11. Transfer the strips into a bowl.
12. In the same skillet, cook the remaining bison flank steak strips.
13. Serve the bison flank steak and vegetables in the tortillas topped with salsa and sour cream.
14. Serve with the lime wedges and Guacamole Salad
15. For guacamole salad in a bowl, mix together the tomatoes, green onions, 1 jalapeño pepper, 2 cloves garlic, salt, and pepper.
16. Gently stir in the avocado and serve over the shredded romaine.

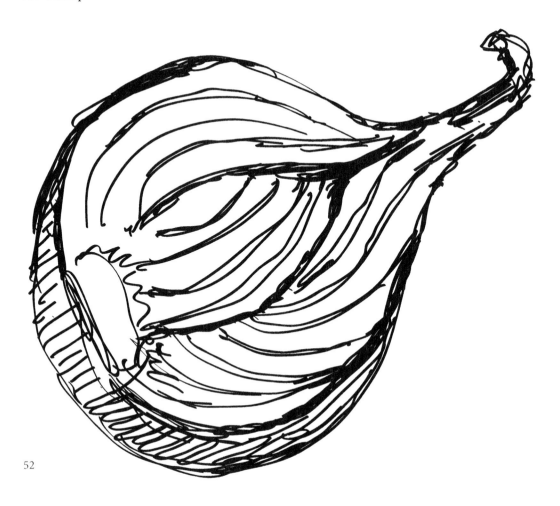

Orange Chili
Beef Fajita Filling

Prep Time: 30 mins
Total Time: 10 hr 50 mins

Servings per Recipe: 4

Calories	234 kcal
Fat	10.7 g
Carbohydrates	16.9 g
Protein	19.4 g
Cholesterol	31 mg
Sodium	1070 mg

Ingredients

1 flank steak
1/4 C. shichimi togarashi (optional)
1/4 C. orange juice
1/4 C. low-soy sauce
2 tbsp lime juice
1/2 orange, zested
1/2 lime, zested
1 tbsp cornstarch
1 tbsp chili powder, or more to taste
1 tsp kosher salt
1 tsp smoked paprika

1 tsp brown sugar
1 tsp cayenne pepper
1 tsp red pepper flakes
1/2 tsp onion powder
1/2 tsp garlic powder
1/2 tsp ground cumin
1 tbsp olive oil
1 onion, cut into slices and separated
1 red bell pepper, cut into thin strips
3/4 C. water

Directions

1. With a meat mallet, flatten the flank steak slightly and rub the shichimi togarashi on both sides of the steak.
2. In a plastic wrap, wrap the steak and refrigerate for 8 hours or overnight.
3. In a resealable plastic bag, mix together the orange juice, soy sauce, lime juice, orange zest, and lime zest.
4. Remove the flank steak from plastic wrap and place in the resealable plastic bag to coat with the marinade.
5. Squeeze out the excess air and seal the bag.
6. Refrigerate to marinate for about 2 hours.

7. Set your outdoor grill for high heat and grease the grill grate.
8. Remove the steak from the marinade and preserve the marinade into a small bowl.
9. Cook steak on the grill for about 8-10 minutes per side, basting with the marinade after every 5 minutes.
10. Cut the steak in half lengthwise and then cut across the grain into thin slices.
11. In a bowl, add the cornstarch, chili powder, salt, paprika, brown sugar, cayenne pepper, red pepper flakes, onion powder, garlic powder and ground cumin and beat till well combined.
12. In a large skillet, heat the oil on medium-high heat and sauté the onion and red bell pepper for about 5-10 minutes.
13. Add the sliced steak, chili powder mixture and water and cook for about 3-5 minutes.

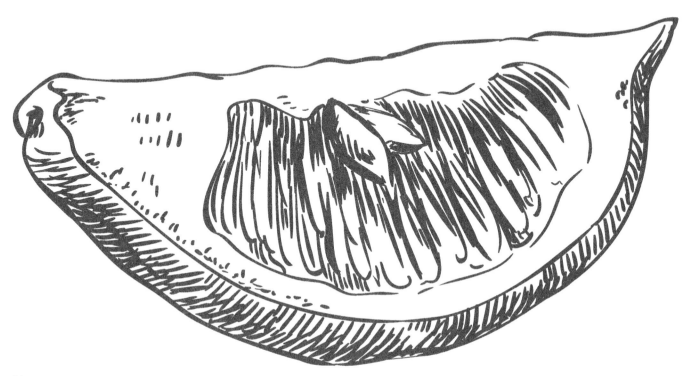

Fajita
Stir Fry

🍲 Prep Time: 10 mins

🕐 Total Time: 25 mins

Servings per Recipe: 4
Calories	98.1
Fat	7.2g
Cholesterol	0.0mg
Sodium	5.4mg
Carbohydrates	8.1g
Protein	1.1g

Directions

1. Cut the beef into 1-inch long and 1/8-inch strips
2. In a skillet, heat 1 tbsp of the oil on high heat and stir fry the beef strips for about 1 1/2-2 minutes.
3. Transfer the beef strips into a bowl.
4. In the same skillet, heat 1 tbsp of the oil and sauté the garlic, onion and green pepper for about 3 minutes.
5. Meanwhile in a bowl, mix together the cumin, lime juice and cornstarch.
6. Add the cornstarch mixture into the skillet and stir to combine.
7. Add the beef strips and stir fry till the mixture is hot and bubbly.
8. Transfer the mixture into a bowl.
9. Serve in tortillas with the desired garnishing.

Ingredients

1 lb boneless lean beef (top round, sirloin)

2 garlic cloves, minced

1 large red bell pepper, cut into strips

1 large onion, thinly sliced and separated

3 tbsp lime juice

2 tbsp oil

2 tsp cumin

1/2 tsp cornstarch

flour tortilla

avocado

tomatoes

salsa

sour cream

cheese

FAJITA
Burgers

Prep Time: 15 mins
Total Time: 25 mins

Servings per Recipe: 4
Calories   351.0
Fat   12.8g
Cholesterol   78.3mg
Sodium   520.1mg
Carbohydrates   30.8g
Protein   29.1g

Ingredients

1/4 C. tomatillo salsa
2 tbsp avocados, chopped
1 tbsp fresh cilantro, chopped
2 slices white bread
1/2 C. onion, finely chopped
1/2 C. red bell pepper, finely chopped
1/2 C. green bell pepper, finely chopped

2 tsp fajita seasoning mix, divided
1/4 tsp salt, divided
1 tbsp tomato paste
1 lb ground turkey
1 egg white
4 whole wheat hamburger buns, toasted

Directions

1. In a small bowl, mix together the tomatillo salsa, avocado and cilantro and keep aside.
2. In a food processor, place the bread slices and pulse till a coarse crumb forms measure 1 C
3. Grease a large nonstick skillet with the nonstick spray and heat on medium-high heat.
4. Add the onion and bell peppers and sauté for about 5 minutes.
5. Stir in 1/2 tsp of the fajita seasoning and 1/8 tsp of the salt.
6. Remove from the heat and keep aside to cool.
7. In a large bowl, add 1 C. of the breadcrumbs, onion mixture, remaining 1 1/2 tsp of the fajita seasoning, remaining 1/8 tsp of the salt, tomato paste, turkey and egg white and mix till well combined.
8. With damp hands, divide the turkey mixture into 4 (3/4-inch thick) patties.
9. Grease the same skillet with the nonstick spray and heat on medium heat.
10. Add patties and cook for about 4 minutes per side.
11. Place 1 patty on bottom half of each bun and top with 1 1/2 tbsp of the salsa mixture.
12. Cover with the remaining half of the bun.

Mexican
Potato Fajitas

Prep Time: 10 mins
Total Time: 35 mins

Servings per Recipe: 4
Calories   149.6
Fat   7.1g
Cholesterol   0.0mg
Sodium   6.8mg
Carbohydrates   19.9g
Protein   2.3g

Ingredients

1 lb potato
2 tbsp canola oil
2 tsp fajita seasoning mix
1 tsp lime juice

Directions

1. Set your oven to 400 degrees F before doing anything else and line a baking dish with the foil paper.
2. Cut the potatoes into cubes.
3. In a large bowl, add the oil, fajita seasoning and lime and mix till a paste forms.
4. Add the cubed potatoes and stir till the potatoes are well coated with the oil mixture evenly.
5. Transfer the potato mixture into the prepared baking dish.
6. Cook in the oven for about 25-30 minutes.

FAJITA
Penne

Prep Time: 4 hr 30 mins

Total Time: 4 hr 45 mins

Servings per Recipe: 6

Calories	360.8
Fat	3.1g
Cholesterol	3.8mg
Sodium	173.1mg
Carbohydrates	77.0g
Protein	9.2g

Ingredients

1 lb penne pasta, uncooked
1 lb lean steak
1 1/4 C. tomato juice, divided
1/4 C. lime juice
3 garlic cloves, minced
1/2 tsp ground cumin
1/2 tsp crushed red pepper flakes
1 tsp vegetable oil
1 green bell pepper, seeded and cut into thin strips

1 red bell pepper, seeded and cut into thin strips
1 yellow bell pepper, seeded and cut into thin strips
1 C. thinly sliced yellow onion
1 C. nonfat sour cream
1 - 2 jalapeno pepper, seeded and minced
1 C. shredded reduced-fat cheddar cheese (optional)

Directions

1. Slice the steak diagonally across the grain into 1/4-inch strips.
2. Place steak in zip-top plastic bag with 1/2 C. of the tomato juice, lime juice, garlic, cumin and red pepper flakes.
3. Refrigerate to marinate for at least 4 hours.
4. Cook the pasta according to package's directions.
5. Meanwhile, remove the steak from the bag and discard the excess marinade.
6. Grease a large skillet with the cooking spray.
7. Add oil and heat on high heat and sear the steak for about 3 minutes.
8. Transfer the steak into a bowl and keep warm.
9. Grease the skillet with cooking spray and sauté the pepper strips and onion till crisp tender.
10. Drain well and transfer in a large bowl.
11. Add steak, pepper mixture, sour cream, jalapeño, remaining 3/4 C. of the tomato juice, salt and pepper and toss to coat.
12. Serve immediately with a sprinkle of the shredded reduced-fat Cheddar cheese.

Fajita
Casserole

🥄 Prep Time: 20 mins
🕐 Total Time: 50 mins

Servings per Recipe: 8
Calories   411.7
Fat   12.7g
Cholesterol   64.7mg
Sodium   118.1mg
Carbohydrates   45.0g
Protein   27.5g

Ingredients

1 1/2 lbs lean ground beef
2 garlic cloves, minced
1 green bell pepper, coarsely chopped
1 red bell pepper, coarsely chopped
1 lb elbow macaroni
1/2 C. sliced green onion, divided
1 tsp ground cumin

1/8-1/4 tsp cayenne pepper
2 (15 1/2 oz.) jars salsa con queso
1 C. crushed tortilla chips, divided
3/4 C. shredded colby-monterey jack cheese
1 tsp chopped cilantro

Directions

1. Set your oven to 350 degrees F before doing anything else and lightly, grease a 13x9-inch baking dish.
2. Heat a large skillet and cook the beef, peppers and garlic till browned completely.
3. Drain the grease from the skillet.
4. Meanwhile cook the macaroni according to package's directions.
5. Drain well.
6. Add the cooked macaroni into the beef mixture with 1/4 C. of the green onions, seasonings, salsa con queso and 1/2 C. of the crushed chips and mix.
7. Transfer the beef mixture into the prepared baking dish.
8. Top with the remaining 1/2 C. of the crushed tortilla chips and remaining 1/4 C. of the green onions.
9. Sprinkle with the cheese and cilantro evenly.
10. Cook in the oven for about 30 minutes.

BACK-TO-SCHOOL
Fajitas

🥄 Prep Time: 15 mins
🕐 Total Time: 35 mins

Servings per Recipe: 4
Calories	223.7
Fat	11.8g
Cholesterol	43.7mg
Sodium	244.5mg
Carbohydrates	4.1g
Protein	24.1g

Ingredients

12 oz. boneless skinless chicken breasts
4 (8 inch) spinach tortillas
1 tbsp cooking oil
1/3 C. finely chopped onion
1/3 C. finely chopped green sweet pepper
1/2 C. chopped tomato
2 tbsp bottled reduced-fat Italian salad dressing

1/2 C. shredded reduced-fat cheddar cheese
1/4 C. bottled salsa
1/4 C. light sour cream (optional)

Directions

1. Set your oven to 350 degrees F before doing anything else.
2. Cut the chicken into bite-size strips.
3. Wrap the tortillas in aluminum foil and heat in the oven.
4. In a 12-inch skillet, heat the oil on medium-high heat.
5. Add the chicken, onion and green pepper and cook for about 2-3 minutes.
6. Remove from heat. Drain well.
7. Stir in the tomato and salad dressing.
8. Fill the warm tortillas with the beef mixture and roll up tortillas.
9. Serve with cheese, salsa and sour cream.

Portobello
Onion Pepper Fajitas

🥣 Prep Time: 8 mins
🕐 Total Time: 14 mins

Servings per Recipe: 4
Calories	255.6
Fat	7.3g
Cholesterol	0.0mg
Sodium	405.4mg
Carbohydrates	40.7g
Protein	8.2g

Directions

1. Heat 1 tsp of the oil in each of 2 skillets on medium-high heat.
2. In 1 skillet, add the mushrooms and cook for about 4 minutes, stirring occasionally.
3. Stir in the balsamic vinegar and cook for about 2 minutes.
4. In another skillet, add the peppers and cook for about 6 minutes, stirring occasionally.
5. Transfer the mushrooms onto a cutting board and slice them.
6. Stir the seasoning and 1/3 C. of the water into the pepper mixture and cook for about 1 minute.
7. Roll up with peppers and onions in lettuce-lined tortillas.
8. Serve with a garnishing of the sour cream and cilantro.

Ingredients

2 tsp oil
4 large portabella mushrooms, stems removed
2 medium bell peppers, sliced
1 medium onion, sliced
1 (1 1/8 oz.) packets fajita seasoning mix
1 tbsp balsamic vinegar (optional)
8 lettuce leaves
8 soft taco-size flour tortillas, warmed
sour cream (to garnish)
fresh cilantro stem (to garnish)

FAJITA STYLE
Lasagna

🥣 Prep Time: 25 mins

🕐 Total Time: 45 mins

Servings per Recipe: 5

Calories	447 kcal
Fat	24 g
Carbohydrates	33.2g
Protein	23.2 g
Cholesterol	79 mg
Sodium	899 mg

Ingredients

1 lb. lean ground beef
1 (1 oz.) package taco seasoning mix
1 (14 oz.) can peeled and diced tomatoes with juice
10 (6 inch) corn tortillas
1 C. prepared salsa
1/2 C. shredded Colby cheese

Directions

1. Set your oven to 350 degrees F before doing anything else.
2. Heat a large skillet on medium-high heat and cook the beef till browned completely.
3. Stir in the taco seasoning and tomatoes.
4. In the bottom of a 13x9-inch baking dish, arrange half of the tortillas evenly.
5. Place the beef mixture over the tortillas evenly.
6. Place the remaining tortillas over the beef mixture and top with the salsa, followed by the cheese.
7. Cook in the oven for about 20-30 minutes.

ENJOY THE RECIPES?

KEEP ON COOKING
WITH 6 MORE FREE COOKBOOKS!

Visit our website and simply enter your email address to join the club and receive your 6 cookbooks.

http://booksumo.com/magnet

https://www.instagram.com/booksumopress/

https://www.facebook.com/booksumo/

Printed in Great
Britain
by Amazon

31926418R00038